Galley of the Beloved in Torment

Galley of the Beloved in Torment

poems by

Kyle McCord

Dream Horse Press
California

Library of Congress Cataloging-in-Publication Data:

McCord, Kyle
        Galley of the Beloved in Torment
            p.   cm

                    ISBN 978-1-935716-02-0
                    1. Poetry

10 9 8 7 6 5 4 3 2 1

First Edition

Cover: "Angry Heaven" by Voytek Nowakowski,
        www.voytek-art.com

Table of Contents

Galley of the Beloved in Torment

First Song of the Beloved

You'll Never Leave This Jungle Alive

It is I, your dead pilot, who sits
in the plane's severed head
and communes with the black box
who reads our destiny
with shattered dials.

Information minces from its brow.

Did I dream of interpreting
languages of the inanimate?

Looking back on it,
on my fourth birthday
when the water balloon hit me,
it loved me.
(I think). (It thought)

it was a heart—sloshing, culpable
as it was. And who's to say
that the heart isn't
what we've imagined it to be—

an organ, eons old, yawning fire
and falling from the trees.
Who's to say our old gods
don't haunt us.

It goes without
that they are black boxes, and this is.
And that this surely weighs
on the divine mind.

Necessary Evil

Even on our best days it is the warring
which keeps us sane, the dinosaurs
who plummeted into the tar an ice age ago.
We would not admit this, but we do,
even on our best days, find it difficult
to imagine the room doesn't sigh a little
when we leave. And we leave.
And we think sometimes
that revealing top tonight. Because we
deserve to feel so now and again.

We have to believe these apostrophes
are breath marks, even on our best days. We need
to be hit when we're born and when we eat too fast.
Juggernauts, great green combines move in
the fields around us. Satellites and great heights
make us feel minute. We have a hammer in one hand
and a sacrificial knife in the other. We have a still-burning
candle in one hand and a hat full of names in the other.
We have a strong cry in one and a bewilderment in the other.

We have, even on our best days, a wedding band
on the one hand holding our helplessness in the same.

Boredom Is a Disease of the Western World

The first death was full of glass and froth.
After this, we were free to fold oblong birds
with our newly ephemeral hands;
free to sit or stand, or drape our worries
over our knees.

And when we were summoned for dinner,
the rinds would fall from the table as bladed angels
or patrons saints of this and that:
patron saint of subordinate clauses or patron saint
of paint which clings to clothes after laundering.

Which is to say we were without soil.
Nothing evaporated even when we begged it.
All our wild things became chairs or ambulances
or little insects lapping out of our palms.
The rivers were the worst sort of gossips.

We would gather beneath the tree trim with clocks,
the mechanical work of time buzzing behind our eyes.
How could we ever be beautiful? we would say,
or how could we shackle the stars? After this, a black seam began
opening above us. And that was the second death.

On Order of Arrival

What we remember of arriving was a sense we'd fought
elsewhere and therefore owned this.
A lock-jawed bird on a dim-lit wire. An unconsidered math
happening around us, to us. Someone slapping us in the face
or ribs, someone shouting for passports.
Was an ax cutting crashes into the treeside.

It's a small-scale apocalypse to the grove, the ax.
And isn't every end just an end to what we know?
No, what's packed at the plant doesn't become again
as organism and what goes undocumented, how could it be
big as a man?

Means intentionality.   Means it matters: the bird, the stumps,
disintegrating gray mushrooming from the refinery.
Or us, the new nature, surrounded by subordinates
and afraid. With our trysts of industry lazily adrift,
on occasion passing through the muddy, shallow streams.

We heard the hammering of voices. Angry.
Someone invoking us like a country or curse. Not of origin.
Someone shouting for order. Order. Of property's
insistence on arrival and exit, which always
was inalterable. And moves us, now, makes us.

We Lay in the Burnt Down Grass

It was clear we were left behind.
Unprescribed. Scribeless.
Our hearts were bent like a wave.
Our hearts were broken unevenly.
Did remorse seem possible? Yes,
we had our haunts. We were given many
lungs. We were asked to describe
our loved ones. Point them out
in the line-up, they said. They kept
bringing coffee. We were asked
to line-up. Select yourselves,
we were instructed. I couldn't
define electromagnetism.
Animal-magnetism: bears, heat,
something about oxidation?
No one wished this on themselves,
they said. But here it is.
Love this. Cherish this.
Bend this over,
and examine it more fully.
You were like us once. You
lived inside a time capsule.
Your name was Lucinda. You
had three children.

We Leave the Land of Our Fathers

They made me leader,
(and I was the fittest leader)
because I stayed up nights worrying
we'd eat bark all winter.

Close to the summit,
witnessing
the campfires of others
in that passive, bewildered manner
of the early-old, the imbecile.

I would say, *You're*
a cigarette extinguished
in my arm.

You would say,
A hundred years seems sensible.
So we went on fighting
for what felt like it.
(Or longer?)

A purple rash rushed
from nettles. Ahead or back
like an oxen in heat.

They made me leader.
Then I was captured by enemies

and what a relief that was,
needing only to carry
out the small acts of life.

It's out of my hands, I would say.
The river meanders, I would
and it would,
and it makes its way;
little hills in the air as it goes.

He Tries to Bury the Rifle but Can't

Then the boy says,
Forget you even bore me.
A hand covers me in clay.
The boy tries to crumble
away the war but can't.

The sky so moldered.
Tell me, boy, why I dream
of wasps then worms,
then the olive hill
pinned back with flames.

But the boy taps once my side
as if in a code,
as if to himself.
And sometimes (I feel) we are alone,

the boy and I. He sways
me into the air, my mouth
gushes slugs.

When His Time Comes, He Fashions a Mannequin

When his time comes, he fashions a mannequin
and attaches a hundred falcons to her arm.
He hooks sequins to the threads of her clothes,
harvests up bits of broken bottles—
thighs. Flowing canvases (smeared slightly),
works of the dead masters, hang from her ears.

Whose voice she has, no one is sure
since the man stores his grief here.
Certainly, it's a lovely grief.
Her feelers sway as she speaks.
Her hair is some number of holy books.
Her genitals, though no man's seen them,
still highly prized.

She's lovely, the mannequin
(who you've unraveled is also an ark).

And by this,
she becomes immeasurably large,
unlovably so.

The titan stands at the end of the country,
calling and cutting her arms with stones.
The man sits on his stump and thinks, and distantly,
his memory is a dog rotting along a road.
And, distantly, you turn the sea gold.

Galley of the Beloved in Torment

And we are given into the hands of the First Beloved that
the broken lifts might light again. That the slave ship leaves
port. That the mercantile act might again act.
As a replacement. That the gift given might not rest
lightly in a mind's given dust. In the lift called monogamy.
Not break nor give in to fits of epilepsy. Like rain or one left
in rain.

The Beloved to whom we are given offers neither tibia
nor tongue. To replace those we have lost.
Each error, individually, (even the act of the error accessed)
must be taken as a gift, in stride. The lethal act of the
Beloved to I, or I to mosquito, or mosquito to skin cell,
or the lethal act of literacy to slavery, the trade of arms.

The First Beloved preens above the neon grave of the heart.
Scientists soon will unlock the mind. First Beloved, your gifts
of rain, of truck overturned, turned over, returned. Of tongue
unfolded like laundry, humps of sand above breakers.

The sky's cracked heart is lightened and pressed
open to the multitudes. A broken elevator opens
in the mind of the epileptic. And one is given into the hands
of the beloved in fire, and in sickness, and in a great boat where
one rows toward the Beloved, unarmed, dreading, aflame.

Fables of the Beloved

Spirit Animal

Laura said, back then, the clouds had two heads.
One, the Norse faces we often see
leaving our hotel rooms, the other
a cool face hanging above the ocean.
There is no definable reason this is true.
That the blue of the waves we see is like, but not the same as,
the blue of our eyes does not make us destined
for some inescapable greatness. Often, the barbed fences
shave the furrows, and we think to ourselves
about long-term lawn maintenance.
But Laura has led me down this road before;
men in uniforms come to me weeping from the forest.
The antelope are looting, burning, will not be reasoned with,
they wail. An electric cowgirl cries in the distance. Laura looks
at me, my beard glinted with beads of sweat. The brands
of my former life begin to overtake my limbs.
A bandana tied around my head. Laura says this day was the
first day
she saw my skin. I remember how my eyes were numb with a
feral animation. I could feel the hot breath of one rock
on another. Careful, I set one paw out into the woods.
The second face of a cloud appeared.

A Mortal Sin

1.

The world to come appeared briefly in the eye of the doll. I was young then and the clouds were called curses, a thin drift of lashes coated the earth. The heart of my youth was bumpy and fat with blood. Tribes of telephone lines wandered the lover's lanes. Of the city, only a strength of idea remained. Soon, we forgot the idea and the angels. The sound of tin guns expired in our ears.

2.

Here is my son and the feral god on whose belly he was birthed. What divine word can help him now? His scalp is sown with weeds. His hands are the frowzy mitts of a mongrel. The calliope of a deity ever echoes in his skull. I remember as a child, how I carried my own torch to the audience of stalks. The field promised me want and I wanted. I was a son of a beekeeper. I was a thief. So I did what I had to do. So I took the blade it gave me. Before me, the wind chanted against the grass, the doll descended onto the altar.

3.

The wolf and the reminder to disregard autumn. The wolf and the beginnings of a god trickling like a riven gorge. The eyes of the doll were everywhere and upon me, so I hid what I had done. In the world to come, may justice trundle after me as it does the wolf. May it follow my trail of urine and afterbirth. When I struck the wolf, I did as my training taught. I did not panic. I stepped from my vehicle. I stooped, looked into his pupils. *We are the same*, he said, *We are undone.*

4.

I panted on into hunger. My hands were snakes in the prairie grass. Later my bruises smelt of blackberries, and I was glad of it. The mortal wolf with its wide-eyed night stick descended into the wild aims of art. It was all a trap though: the painted stones, the silence. The judge raised a single, reticent arm, but the crowd would not be quieted. He had the corrosive smile of a doll. He washed his hands with lacquer.

The Beastman Poems

Every dream is a wet dream. My brothers were hard but feral. At ten, hair appeared above my navel. A sheep was taken hostage by cruelly-lit neighbors. Father taught brother to use the yard. Mother punished my seven bad postures. A ransom note collected dust. My musk threatened father. A tape of the sheep's execution arrived on our doorstep. All our best toys fell from my brother's mouth. Father ate my musk with a stone. Brother filled the sky with hissing cats. Brother hid centerfolds of half-eaten antelope. Dreams drew their stiff witness. Our pelts were pursed for velocity. Our teeth were sharpened by lamplight. We were told to visit the neighbors.

Father's laws were the stones caught in our spokes. Father presupposed all the traits of a smiling lawyer: strict discipline, rigid facial definition, angle of eyes, wet sallow eyes, toughened forepaws, soft pads of back paws, predatory angle of skull, jaws able to carry nearly a ton of carcass, long tongue protruding, shaded maw muscle, firm mandible. A mark was drawn above our doorframe. My sister dawdled while out for milk. Small bowls were placed before our befuddled eyes. A demonstration was enacted and our futures distinctly outlined. The light grew greasy settling on our panes and the creases of our spines.

It was in the becoming we learned not to stutter. Father bought me the Beastman figure to reveal God's reckless kindness. A sort of spiritual sidestepping became necessary. A kettle was brought to boil. *The genus of wilderness is the concubine of greatness,* intoned mother. Father's head kept nodding uncontrollably. Better days were swept into the dull shadow of autumn. Worse days were drowned in the dark of our closets. Birds landed on live wires. Birds fell from the air as pies. Birds' bones muttered in the underbrush. Mother had on her cooking apron. And there we were: barking at the earth.

Father hid Beastman in the linen closet. On the third day he rose from the closet bathed in radiance. His grave clothes were covered in sulfur and we could see through the bladed glass of his eyes. One hand had been molded into a sign of peace and the other held the scruff of a live cerebrus. *Behold,* he said, *the oft forgotten left hand of God.* Children love this sort of thing. Children love to pee in the ocean. Children love the dark descent into the forest and the shimmering creature rushing ahead. The forest was obscure and full of half-horse men. The forest was full of lit torches and music so I turned back. On the way home I hummed the songs with which the playground children would later taunt me. The hotels were illuminated with stories. Flocks of hookers gathered on the lake.

Humming to Myself in a Voice I'd Never Heard

You have to cease believing
the world will end tomorrow.
On the cabinet's ligneous surface,
the parking tickets marshal,
letters not-so-subtly hostile—
movies you refuse to return.
Morbid thoughts catch
in your whirlpool of unemployment:
Into the ballroom of the west you came waltzing
and into the strip mine of death—
You race this banner through
your cerebrum enough and, bam,
all the ducks dead from arsenic.
Evidently some company named Anaconda,
and for weeks representatives arrive
in the neighborhood like a smell of rotten eggs.
Each one wears a hardhat hung too low
and enacts for you
how the arsenic found its way
into Plummer's Pond.
It's perfectly safe now,
they say. But no one really lets it go.
They look on dubiously,
hands on hips.
And you don't know what to think.
You're killing your mother.

What Can Only Be the Seventh Circle

Only one fork in the cabinet,
so you drop it down a well.
The fork hits a cobble
like a lisp of gunfire.
We wait. We peer.
And on this goes for years.
An old fable tells of two friends
who coax a horse down a well.
They send down a letter,
to no avail.
One friend cuts off his ear,
but the horse won't utter a syllable.
So selfish! Then one of the friends
is drafted and dies.
His mother refuses interview
and stands daily by the well.
One day the horse asks,
"Woman, why are you crying?"
"Horse, my son has died,
and I have nothing for which to hope."
"Woman," says the horse,
"there are many heavens
on this earth, some as small
as the moss I lap from the cobbles.
All my legs are broken, but each day
a hundred paradises engulf me."
Later, the woman boards up the well
knowing the horse
has killed her son.

Born from Crags, the Miniature Must Struggle On

The next day, the President finds the leaves fallen from the bonsai tree.
Too late for watering. The little foliage left withered to a sickly mint.

He glances in the mirror. He flexes. A lazy heat is breaking outside.

The President calls Leo. In the parlor, they look over the bonsai:
where it turns, how it turns. Leo suggests making a plastic copy of the tiny tree.

The President takes a Polaroid. Leo copies the Polaroid.
Yes, Mr. President. Leo is handing out photos to all the servicemen.

Forty-five minutes later, the bell rings. The President's girlfriend is here. She's
wearing her sweatband and jogging shorts. Let's go for a run. Then everyone is changing.

Dewy sweat starches the lawns. Out on the run,
the President's girlfriend talks about her dream.

Something had gone wrong.

You were dead. Everyone was panicking. I kept slipping
into boxcars then I'd wake and we'd be somewhere else.

The more I rode, (she coughs) the less I remembered.
Like every day was the beginning of something I'd never meant to start,

never thought I could.
I'd wake, find myself on another train.

They pass the Italian restaurant the President likes.
When they get home, everything is as it was.

She examines the bonsai as she always does. He's getting big, she says. Flickers of passersby press the edges of his vision. The area outside the gate fills.

Yes, replies the President.

The Princess, the Boar, the Moon

A tradition from the old faith, once yearly, the reigning princess would present herself before the people, the paparazzi, the bog dwellers. She would bow once to the west, once to the east, daub her golden hair with mud, turn to kiss the country's ugliest boar. Her servants, despite their dislike of the ritual, dutifully selected the animal, and no one would have dared to question their selection; a crown of flies circled its ass. The creature was cockeyed. Its snout: one of nature's least savory works.

A man was to lie with his wife and take in the spectacular affair each year on the television. Usually, the princess would never see the boar again. She would sign her edicts, shop for plums or dog food in the village below. One Sunday, she spied a boar eyeing her outside the grocery. It cowered behind the wheel of a Saturn, its shriveled face reflecting not rage, not sadness or pity.

This would all have sieved away easily enough, had she not been reminded by the sound of hoof beats leaving the royal infirmary later that night. "Arthur," said the princess to her serf, "do you love me?" "Ma'am, do I not pull the figs from the branches and burn to the ground the barns of your enemies?" "Yes," replied the princess. "Perhaps what I mean to ask is this: to what factory will the wind someday go? And what is to be done with the terrible contentment?"

The moon had orbited back, doting on the wall as if it belonged there. The long table pulled the moon onto plates. The shine of it illuminated a sandbag factory across the freshly sprinkled lawn. It was a night when the very electrons of the arm seemed uneasy, insatiable. Then Arthur began to speak.

On Return to the Ship

There were a whole tribe of us from the East come through
the turnstile. For a while I walked beside a family of four.
Then an old man; then he died. Then a cow on a line
and a farmer. I could say some things about the going,
though it's nothing you couldn't assume:
diving insects haunted me, I had a knife for protection.

I felt, at times, I'd achieved the end of my life.
Someone would get up to a high place, amount a theory.
I'd listen attentively. Things would get better
or my standards would lower, and eventually they'd get old
or a gunman or disease would fade them from view.
A freighter would foam from the mist,
and winds would batter it back to the sea.

Any bearing of this has since been lost to me.
But could I have any of it again, I'd have the cow,
the hope to embark on a plane and wind up somewhere
utterly impractical: Fiji, Kuala Lumpur, wherever.
I pondered escape of course, obsessed over it even
but it's the consistency of any action that spurs it on.
Magicians will go, night after night,
performing acts after audiences have gone.

That's how what happens happens. The magic of this time
languishes next to the magic of the next time.
One sees in the sky-lit cat a sleep towards which we are moving
and wonders how to board such a vessel
which orphaned us so many moons before.

Venus Clothed by Distance

Originally arising from sash—*fashion*—
or a fondness for softness
typically associated with women.

During the era of Italian city states,
rural debtors described the princely
passions of dress as *sashioni*
only in the occlusion of their campfires.
This, like most derisions, was later adopted affirmatively
by the rising families of Apulia and inner-Rome.

As the word migrated
to the western estates of Kiev,
plague traveled at its side, twining
with the proto-Russian, *falluck*: to depart
or to turn a jar till all contents, typically gypsum,
reach a single end.

The connection between the two terms bore:
one which dies each season and rises with alms,
the current understanding of Russian fashion.

Then mighty Europe lapsed into its sleep of war.

Nowadays, we know
(or believe we know)
what perpetuates even after upheaval—
famine, flu epidemics.

Fashion became a means to reorder death
and life as baptism had been hundreds of years before:

beauty in its time then
the slow plod toward subsequent existence.

Americans have challenged such notions of the recursive
as the cornerstone of fashion,
arguing in favor of *saffion*, from the Portuguese,
a sometimes troubled clothing of the eternal,
as the true root.

The term's lineage traces to usage during the Roman Empire
to delineate the life of a soldier
from the immortal being of the emperor.

This is why American models are asked to refuse tattoo,
why fashion is so often associated with the search
for dark matter
which would evidence an ever-expanding universe,
though no evidence seems to suggest such.

Because the young hold such sway
in American fashion,
the fetish of the perpetual I surfaces.

They insist upon it like a mantra. A people unfazed
even faced with the inevitable,
though their land is stubborn and ill-suited
for the uninterrupted.

Such is the state of things in America.

Against Adaptation

Most evolutionary models posit the implant of dinosaur remains
on the earth by an evil presence around 1200 AD.
Given this, the devil likely sculpts till the wee hours of the morning.
Menace—as the maker of things—makes sense enough to us.
Tribal societies often eat the first-born to enhance fertility.

Why does symmetry of structure define what a woman says
to a man she meets at a dinner party—botanical garden, beautiful
fireworks seen from bridge? (Flame-colored lotus, I love you.)
This also could be a theory—the rubber tree, its survivability
in the face of shopping center decline.

Other possible evolutionary models include: Dangling Constant Theory,
Constellation, Black Lake, Bobbing Flora Model,
Unintelligible or Ox and Cart Design,
Theman, Thomas, and Neel's Axioms of Intent.

The Hand on Heater Theorems,
The Graceful Dancer, Virgin Paradox,
Microbe Velocity Theory, as well as
the less favored Hungry Hippo, Marble Earth Hypothesis.

Each year, we grow closer as a country by the symmetry of our features.
The face of the president shines occasionally from the ether
of television. To save us from the guilt of inaction and the homeless
sun turns. How has the bark we grow grown so thick? Not history
or poetry. Praetorianism, the underground, and you, always, the Evil One.

Like a Hive Where Sleep Is Kept

A man drinks a bottle of bleach. Suddenly the man and bleach do not know each other, as if both were born in that same bronzed instant with the dryer gleefully twittering away in the basement, the day beckoning beautifully from the window. Now the man goes out into the midst of the day.

The bleach rolls about. The bleach stares out of the fishbowl of the man's stomach. It envies the man's easy ways: the man's daydreams of being a sparrow or hammer, the day's mandreams of being a bulldozer. The bleach dreams of being a bird feeder hanging from a tree. The man goes to the office which is like a tree only it's concrete and nothing grows from it. The day grows older and closes about the blocks of the city.

The life of a day, thinks the bleach, *is like the moths with its imparting of dust and moldering. Sometimes we find whole days in our closets. Then it is as if we were strangers, alien even in our own light.* The man sits in the humid torpor of the office. The man farts. The bleach is a jackal pup. Outside, the day knits together a womb from which night will come.

Swirling about in the stomach, every thought for the bleach is like a clean wall. The man becomes nauseated with the fatted dreams of the bleach. Every thought for the day is like a balmy rising of yeast. *This is the moment*, vows the bleach, *that we shall finally glimpse each other's faces, man.* The day's water breaks. The bleach leaps from the stripped ripeness of the man's esophagus.

The bleach gasps with joy. The man vomits. The day grows sad and gray. The day envies everything given the man and pours itself out over his writhing body. The bleach is fraught with a wild, unerring love. *Now*, thinks the bleach, *all our worries inflate like a fire of bees.*

A Willful Sort of Suffering

Sometimes I wake on a distant planet
and don't remember what I had for breakfast,
how I came to you years ago.
I could have drunk the whole river
with moths pelting reeds
like opalescent marbles. As we passed
through the drift towns in a truck bed,
your cousin hawking corn.
Then to sleep under the streetlights.
Sometimes the moon vines velvet
around my ankles and they say, *There's no one*
to tell you what to think on this planet.
No tribunes, no temples. All night the clubs pour
drunks from their mouths.
You can imagine how I feel about this.
At home, I sew some pants
while I try to think nothing
of pleasure. I open my mouth—
here come chrysanthemums.

On Singularity

In this century, at least, it's the lone wolf who's loneliest.
If a relation of emotions could be compiled.
We could understand our instinct to order
even the tiniest of forms, our homes,
in which we are infinitely small, infinitely terrifying.

Other theories of the individual could be offered.
How light or a white, sun-lit tree must sense
desertion, as anything with a dual nature must.
Skeletal and divided against its own hunger as it is.
The horse from the hill, brooded over by stars.
The metrical adjustment of grass
winded down to the thinnest blade.

The lone soul we see sometimes,
the imagined self walking down a gravel road,
leans to feel out these unseen actors.
The church leaves shades of resistance made only by its being.

It's identity, we know, duality, by which we are made
most isolate. Overly morose or ignorant and elated,
powered primarily by the visceral. We spend most of our days
cutting sopping carpet out of a basement.

Willing to weather and to pine, to weep and to hazard
gratitude. Like a storm or one lost in storms,
to still, to watch. These imagined boundaries race past each other.
The universe seen from a distance appears to be one wolf
or two wolves run together as if by carelessness.

You Rest Now in the Halls of Your Fathers

There was this show called "Enemies"
where a Golden Lab and Dachshund
ran around in an overgrown field.

The shadows weaving, twine, turning in
the prairie. All subtle manipulations of nature,
of course. Cornea, neural pathways.

A metaphor, maybe. An afterlife.
Some distant contingent of others sentenced
for the betterment of their minds.

Look, my name is Eric Ansen. The year is 1990.
And if you've found this time capsule,
you'll know to trust no one.

A weak historian examines events
and sees a legend of the intimate, an arrow
or error, or sheet, flattened.

But here's how things really are.

A Golden Lab and Dachshund
lie down in a field. And after a long time, you
lie down there too. With your wife, again.
Like me, like everyone.

You know something actual, honest.
Faintly, you can hear the rallies of cannibals.
And the song of fire cows down.
And this also passes.

As if to the Lengthening Hillside

Why go on like this, only hurting yourself?
For you, the cellar stairs remind of injuries incurred.
I am busy climbing my own ladder though,
into something like a loft.
I mean, there is a structure of sorts.
I mean, there are the wind-racked, the snowbound,
images left imperfect, filmed by permafrost.
So if today you find yourself regretting,
bear in mind that I was there first
running birds off the porch, ranting incoherently
at the raccoons thumbing through yesterday's mail.
Which is to say you leave some things out. You do.
Probably with an oath in mind.
Probably curious how the hero feels
nettled with arrows, carrion swabbing the sky.
Measured out, effaced, maybe fearless
in the face of the entering dark. Maybe not.
Look, when the record of the skin is gone,
only the throat plays those somber,
utterly dependable exit notes. Says the foreigner,
You seem more stripped down than I remember:
wilds more vacant, storehouses boarded up,
venom well-concealed in the old and unwanted.
None of us too much wanted, too much to say
about the shades discarded by homes. Smoking
for some reason addiction never fully explains.
Two men roll out a barrel of oil,
up the alley, around a corner, into the warehouse—
Where is this going? When you, the hero you, says
as if to the lengthening hillside,
The bomb bay is opening. Please step to either side.

Leaving those scary parts out,
you declare yourself a person of the book
while thinking neither of people nor books.
Of the belief that you will someday wind up in this desert,
then what could we possibly say to each other?
The black sand dunes rupture like a squid's ink.
The thirst thinking like a rat.
If today, I guide my toes into a sock
then a footed sock into a tangled wood, what good is that?
Farms all vacant, reservoir alight with grub fish
full of something thick as sleep.
Why go on like this
reading the books, returning them?

Song of the Self Divided

It Was a Rat that Carried Your Heart to the Sea

A dusk begins and we return to it.
A sea becomes the question and answers itself.
To be held in a steady gaze and then become roots.
To forget for a time.

The sun sulfated, its steady pulse
playing along the fingers of our garments.
A button. A sock. A voice
and no voice looming from it.

To watch autumn's brown origami.
The cat's ribs clinging to its skin.
Flocks of scissors racing along a coast.
I am sorry for the severed drift of the sea.

To answer was impossible.
To acquaint oneself with lighthouses, griefs.
To as a child divide each thing in its openness.
A steep breathed braying. A boot's roily gills.
To grow sick with smoothness. To be born
an incalculable number. To count to yourself in stones.

You Come Back Over the Stony Field

What is it when passion comes to an end?
From the lecherous men, I bought five dusty cobs.
I cut open my palm shucking the second to last.
Blood matting the lusterless yellow.
The skin tethered back together since then. On the drive
back from the dell, stretches of fertile darkness bridged
town to town. In these pockets, strung together
by the occasional barnlight, the pulsing thrum
of the engine is its own manner of silence.
Like this dissonance of slight noise is unsustainable.
After a period of months, sometimes years, they say
the once novel alchemy of the cerebellum settles—
surprise devolves into easy expectation. A tea cup perches
atop light which greedily reels along the tabletop.
Our patio above the market. Your hair with wind's
architecture moving restless, through.
And for four months we lived
like that. To sleep on the bamboo mats
like we were prisoners in our own city. Eating little,
leaving little. Like the body conceals its weakness
till the strains are too great. To be salvaged.
I feel now for where my seams have formed,
the valley behind breaking up miles of onyx.
The month of oranges and no money for oranges.

Leslie Vegetative

The brumes roll back and back like an unending coma.
The plane flies from one end of the pool to the other, evaporates.
The whole shallow world carries on like this, Leslie—
I drive towards the artesian gates and they part like a man's hair,
the practiced finger points at an x-ray then feels for cigarettes.
Rust slows. A slow russet overtakes the night.
Please wake, Leslie. The world is almost over, and if everything is real,
film clacking against the reel, the waves emptying
out along the shore…Lately, the trees seem crucified by frost,
laughing and laughing then crossing themselves, then burning like effigies.
My thoughts circle this scene, calling and calling as if they were a thing,
an intruder; in the dream, you wake up, look around. It's me,
the lion child, the golden doctor smoking cloves.
We've saved you. The risen saints are singing in the harbors.
Come see where we watched you emerge from the sea's arm
coated in rut weeds and glycerin, bathed in flame.

How One Door Opens into Another

This is how I knew you were good:
that I did not fall dead in the streets tracked
with bike skids,
that as I passed the towering rush of seasons
and sidewalks, my hair was blown glass and goldenrod.

Salt would overtake the snow.
Floods of ice or burrowing animals
would lose me whole days, weeks and then crumble.

The railcars would come, a rising smoke
from the brickyard. I would lie and listen
to their sifting in the odd lamps that coved the streets,
how they mixed with the ocher noise
of bells lifted from the old chateau at the center of town.

Like a voice, or a rock bidden into air, chestnuts
would fall and explode against the avenues.
Dogs would strain against their chains.
The sky would pass and leave me aching.

Years carrying on until, my body too heavy
in orbit, hair fenced along my chin, my life
passed along into the cities.

After this there was no more need for years.

With the shuffling of keys, one day opened into another.
The clouds were so many I could not count, and
a crop of fresh rain would fall daily on my face.

The smog of the city curded against it.
At least a hundred clouds encircled my hair.

Slowly We Learn to Save a Little

Corner of midday in a deli. A leaf
of paper off a bottle of blue paint.

Comes the crow too far off to be
a crow, but we can make it out, as we do

old age when we return at last, to childhood.
Out on the porch, at home, at last.

I tell my friends on the phone
if we could see all we'd lost,

we could be again as monks.
They'd bring us a hundred items—

wilted plants, hair's smell in sleep,
clarity which we'd grudgingly abided—

but we'd tell them nothing of our past lives.
We'd fell into our factories and the private

properties and water
from sprinklers would feed us.

Into Disrepair

To believe where the mind resides
the physical being takes no part,
why did I ever take this as gospel?
Water intrudes a lung.

Rot enshrines the home.
A woman with a flower blouse
spoke to an assembly where I was forced
to sit. The dangers of shallow diving.

She had a wonderful tea-green porch,
one could say.
Candles pedestaled on the end table.

Seemingly innocent enough,
the paint turned autumn.
Open the cabinets, close the cabinets.
It keeps people out, these uneasy details.
Add the Masons' half-acre—white,
no windows onto only prairie.

But where's the manor where a body must go?
Easy enough without art to put this off,
let the cardinal levities do and play the off-keyed
piano. Driving with grapes
in a sack because it's a way, where I go.

Loutish river, your laugh fills down on occasion.
But mostly you make me anxious of matters
with nothing to do with you.
Sometimes mercury. Sometimes a bridge.

There Was One Tongue and It Was Forgotten

I live in a house. My closet:
a maze of jars, shoes, a guitar.

Two doors down a sign warns,
No trespassing.

The weeks pass;
I go trespassing.

Always I feel
along the ceiling for cracks.

Always a child, I wake,
root beneath the pillow to find a sliver of myself

gone,
coins in its stead.

In the morning, many languages
—unlearnable method of radiance.

The quiet exchange of objects. Basket to tub.
Garden to dandelion.

Figures playing along the window. Now drapes
clothing the gust. Now me tapping along the sill

in an unfamiliar parlance. It reminds me
of something shattered into ornateness.

It reminds me of something swept up
and tumbled out on a beach.

How I Am Made Better Through Struggle

To paint. To break the daily objects down:
fruit, stand, fan of space spreading
childlike and dazzlingly played upon the water.
To see these symbols and then to wait
to be seen by doctors
as if through a vast series of lenses.

Often, I sense the crowding heat of others—
the daguerreotype machine pumps out its inspired image,
the science books won't shut up.
I consider you a miracle
heart which has survived all this
and daily indicates: yes, there must be bread.
Yes, there must be oils, pastels.
The great body must plunge onward
or the volcanoes will find themselves
the only ones decorating the atmosphere
for pictures untaken. Abstracts unfinished.

And though this town might tell you otherwise,
consequence can still bind us,
even after the solar structures wrack and crumble.
Beyond this world extends an expanse of seas and sea-
stippled dunes, and more ropes
than a sane person can break.
If you all day paint as you are told,
someday your snow may even smell of hair.
Physical matter matters, yes.
Though the rapture of the body never dwelt
in a body at all. This capsizes, perishes—
whole rivers famish and die.

Even in Joan, the straw woman, the heart
(also a river) rumbled and demanded rest beyond the dominion.
This must surely tell us something
that the daimyo of organs breaks down into insurrection.

Understand, you carry memory like an oar or brick.
You are getting off one boat and into another
and how heavy the river's hands!

And Mighty Saturn Would Circle Our Heads

Despite what we imagine, the bullets of our doings do return.
So certain our individuality would be the one sun
by which astronomy was instructed. But, in short,
these emotions aren't anyone's in particular.
Aren't entered in by wire or gate or westward glance.

The streetlights snap into view above suburbs,
and for a moment, our concentration breaks.

Seems we'd lived carelessly, unaware of our living even as it
occurred.

Someone would make a sandwich, and we'd eat it.
Someone would stain glass, and we'd walk through that glass.
Walking through panes as we walk across dunes—enamored,
heart-strung, half-asleep. With our constant friends:
limping wind, the dog hedged by darkness, darkness.

Because the forcibly unswerving cannot betray.
When we were young, a dulcimer would try a den
of light and cloud hung above a bay. Gray no-ones
would move about us and this song, ours only,
we clenched between our knuckles, hid even from ourselves.
For twenty-two years, we would wake, eat, go to work
never knowing our movements were charted
by whatever thin light this rhythm offered.
What plan could be devised, seen from so great a distance.

And where this light might be leading us.
What would be made by what's made to remain.
A few speculated wights. Some houses looted by rain.

Poem in the Shape of a City

All you remember of yourself
smells of absinthe.
The sky with light,
the sky splotched with decrepit light.
All you remember,
your whole life,
bursts into rewind
in the machine's mouth.
Only your head has been shaved,
only death thinks of itself
as a street you have entered,
drawn and redrawn
by coal colored hands.
In the film, black and white,
which follows,
you and I,
too old, too silent,
vanish beneath a furnace.
When a temple appears
we demand a hundred years
before its furious lamps.
We are like ourselves,
and so ungrateful.
So we keep crying out.
Your lips are backwards.
And death thinks of itself
as a collector of pedigrees.
It is late, far too late:
the moon is a clock hand
moving against the tide.
The sea bares its back.

The Celestial Fish Pared by Stars

Cold barge, you're leaving over the plains of sea salt and algae.
A sugar of moonlight wrinkling the air above the waves
you break. Your bow. Your phantom mansions adorned
and how the furnace of your lungs breathes back iron,
dust. Everything broken before the industry you are.

Cold barge, could I separate myself from you?
The way the city is only a part of the city. As if the streets
could peel back to show new signs or clotheslines then close
again, around us, a crowd of forms swelling, drowning us out.
The incredible act of humility we know must happen,
must be happening elsewhere. Past the electric ports.
Ghost towns, foreign even to phantasms.

In the unwritten story of our lives, we row out
to the edge of the world. The sea yowls itself black, snapping
at the oars of the skiff. Distantly, the future behemoths
of glass and light lie unbent. And we, made more
ourselves, scream, as if in a mania. We hammer the deck
with a spear. The dust rises, animate. Into a man.

We are asked to don estrangement as a god must.
The weight of knowledge which takes on water.
I think more, black barge, on mortality's selfish wish.
How an albatross cuts the jet stream
its majesty undiminished by routine.

I wonder more into the dream summer offers.
With everything, the Colby, the yard, only as it is
to the senses. Extricable, unexaggerated.
How we were children once in summer, awoken

by David Berkowitz and divided into two vessels.
How by each waking we are divided further
and given another in our likeness.

Final Song of the Beloved

Everything Is Gathering

It is gathering.

In the yard, the leaves from the trees
and the light that leaves the trees
and the light that remains.
And the light that remains settles only a second
on a nest, then settles somewhere
like an unseen hand.

And the wind that lashes the streets
and the streets that brush out between cities
and the cities that rush with a rolling oil
of asphalt. And the asphalt is heated
and gathers like our bodies knotting together in their old
and droning ways. They are gathering, our bodies.

The peoples with their visions and maps,
with their statuses and their statues,
with their coins and their curling irons,
and their overcoats. With their crossing of bridges,
their climbing of stairs, their washing of hair
in the dark of the morning,

their thinning, their fattening,
their putting on of clothing,
and their ending and beginning of days
and the various names by which they are known
and will someday be remembered by a marble tablet
that speaks to the earth.

With their skin timid in tried seasons.

And their seasons which are more than we can bear
to count so they are remembered by the names
of others who have run off to countries that have no name.
And the countries cannot be named.
The seasons cannot be named. They cannot be named.
And they are gathering.

And the thousand stars by which
we have sworn; all vowels
and vows and seamless and building exchanges.
The markets full with barley and wine
and the smell of finely fermented soap from the east.
With its winds and its gods,
its scimitars and its sands and its crates.
Its exchanges of gold and its palaces of gold
and its boulevards of gold and dust and flame
and the slight and fleeting smell of incense
rising and falling in the etches of shadows.

A frost is gathering on the windows.
A blood is gathering on the butcher's floor.
And all the animals are gathering with Orpheus.
And in the untamed place, Orpheus gathers up the galaxies,
the swirling universes and their empty spaces and their dark matters.
It is darker than our darkest pans or the charcoal
that gathers from our fires. A fire gathers in the wires
crowning the city and in the gutters crowded with leaves.
And it is gathering in the rat holes and in the dumpsters.

And on the winded roads and on the worn billboards,
the words form into gaggles and fly.

From the words our nations emerge
as if from a body of water.
Our nations with their leveled weapons and their laws,
their tiled kitchens and their empty kitchens
and their alleys and alcoves and bars with bearded men
who gather balls and scatter them like bandits.
They are gathering, the bandits are gathering.

And the seas and the rocks stringing the seas.
And the bees with their savage buzzing and
the beautiful buzzing that rises with the city streets.
And the trees who have wept
every season and have heard our every word
and our wisdom and borne it admirably.
They are gathering.

The town with its wizened ways,
its rising and setting suns and its settling down
and its greening lawns and pruned trees. We are gathering
and in the gathering becoming strangers. The strangers
are gathering in the wild dark of the woods with its
masks and axes and its new and unlived lives.
The locusts and the mildews and the seas and the graves
beyond and within the seas are like scarecrows.
A white wave with its foam is distantly gathering.
The crows of the field, they are settling on our shoulders.
They are gathering and they are pecking at our eyes;
they are teaching us the way across the sea and they
are carrying us in their beaks. They are building us small
arks in their minds and they are as thick as a sky.

Against Such Magnitudes

Afternoon strips to wallpaper
on a lake dusted in millet.
You pocket a grotto
through a hole in the water.

A mere child,
you fancy yourself a mystic,
dancing bear that you are.

"Soon," you say,
"I will strip off my bear also.
One hand will soap another.

A crow will come
(like this one)
a cigarette burn to the sky,
to take me to a lake,

and there the reel
of my life will sing
and slow.

The golden thread.
The polestar molting,
letting us down, at last."

Rites of Passage

I wonder what it is that makes a man,
who nests in the daylight, though the daylight nests
not at all, but goes about with a stiff spine.
Knocking shadows from kiosks.
Surely someone summons morning
with a single honk
while a dog ascends to the speed of cancer
and dies. It's a lesson in permanence, all this,
the animate faces of the recently wed, the frail.

I wonder what it is that makes a man, and makes
him a helmet and hands him a shovel.
To speak of the simple life or the conscience
who possesses neither simplicity nor tenderness.

Who are we more
than a workcrew standing along a highway,
digging up a pipe
to the heart of the city?
The geese we hear may be no more
than the mind, more honest, speaks.

I wonder what sort of meteor it began as, the mind,
and who recorded its desiccating re-entry,
and what it is that makes a man.

Then We Saw the Coil of Stars

On the last day, Abraham lay down his hacksaw and sander.
Neighbors trudged to cars as if toward a great incline, ineffable.

It's the historians who say Abraham walked among us.
Abraham ate the lemongrass like any of us.

On the last day, you were the desk you were at, father.
The tower fell like the tower of language. Somewhere a
microphone spoke.
We gravitate to TV as if beset by storm or panic.

Where are we not the black specks of ourselves
seen in the orbital's light?

Abraham picked up and left for his ex. Historians say
that for an instant you will feel yourself
filling the pavement outside the government buildings.

Then the mail service resumes. We say to ourselves,
I saw a second hand from heaven crumple itself. And men…
what mischief, given no order, we'll do.

I saw Abraham lay down his rusted pistol and bullhorn.
All for no sake, father. No easy explanation.

Still Are the Strings of the Ancients

About us, the quality or lack of our luminescence,
we'll never make up our mind.

Evils we do or don't
(little good it does)
refract, depending, as they do,
on our angle of vantage.

The light that does, (the good)
we take for granted:
the yard lit whether we wake it or not.

The light that doesn't,
should it reach our cornea
some night when the ancestors allow,
we would never forget.

But barring these,
minus praise or antipathy,
an object, say a hand
turning a room into view,
continues its present course unabated.

By comparison or resistance,
we become not-our-father,
permitting a part of him to live on
in antithesis
when we were happy enough
to see him surface a last time
from the myriad cancers and go.

We were happy enough
to travel and to be broken
and later to be reconstituted into statues.

To surmise this as bravery
in our friends and to continue on
in the copper heart.

Even if it clangs and knocks,
even if it recognizes no one.

We Hear Only the Snapping of the Crabgrass

All acts of heroism begin: a woman and oxen
hauling ten gallons of water over a mountain
are hauling ten gallons of water over a mountain.

Suddenly it starts to rain
and acts of heroism are the first to leave.
Like leaves operated on by weather,
we're made better, less ourselves.
In an instant able to lift a truck or trunk
of a tree from a loved one.

Call it unaccounted mercies (or cruelties),
passion of the railway on the equine.
The elevators relief to my tendons.

We know innately all once depended
on some idiot with a sharp implement
and that the prophets were unkind
to their daughters, especially.
Abandoned to live a human life,
not so special, not so inexhaustible.

A detritus of blossoms blows by a church.
The town hero hits his daughter
who loves women, for loving women,
while one son inherits the business.
And another son comes over a mountain.
And a bomb explodes in Birmingham.

And we'll never admit (we won't) that decay's
no more than the spirit's unflagging idol.

Who lifts the girders, at last. At its mercy,
we remember little, and wander
out in rain, and no one's grateful enough
for anything.

Acknowlegments

Special thanks to journals, especially those who were kind enough to feature some of these poems.

Poems were featured in:

American Poetry Journal: "There Was One Tongue and It Was Forgotten," "Leslie Vegetative," "You Come Back Over the Stony Field," "Poem in the Shape of a City," "A Willful Sort of Suffering"

Asheville Poetry Review: "A Mortal Sin"

Boston Review: "It Was a Rat that Carried Your Heart to the Sea"

Cimarron Review: "As if to the Lengthening Hillside"

Columbia: A Journal of Literature and Art: "Like a Hive Where Sleep Is Kept"

Drunken Boat: "The Princess, the Boar, the Moon"

Fourteen Hills: "The Boy Tries to Bury the Rifle But Can't"

Gulf Coast: "What Can Only Be the Seventh Circle"

Iowa Poetry Association: "Boredom Is a Disease of the Western World"

Painted Bride Quarterly: "Galley of the Beloved in Torment"

Segue: "We Leave the Land of Our Fathers," "Humming to Myself in a Voice I've Never Heard" "The Little Number Attests" "Venus Clothed by Distance"

Skein: "We Lay in the Burnt Down Grass"

Way-Wiser Press: "Still Are the Strings of the Ancients," "Still Are the Strings of the Ancients."

William and Mary Review: "The Beastman Poems"

About the Author

Kyle McCord was born in Phoenix, Arizona in 1984. He grew up in rural Iowa and attended the Iowa Writer's Workshop and the Program for Poets and Writers at the University of Massachusetts-Amherst, where he received his MFA in 2009. He's received awards or grants from the Academy of American Poets, the Vermont Studio Center, and the Iowa Poetry Society. He currently lives and teaches in Des Moines, Iowa.

About the Cover Artist

Voytek Nowakowski was born in 1959, in a small city called Leczyca, Poland - a city with a thousand year old history and many beautiful castles, old buildings and churches. He started to paint when he was 8 years old - penetrating old buildings and ruins of castles looking for treasures and antiques. One day he found an old box of oil paints and some old paintings. He was charmed by the beauty of historic things and started to collect them, love, and appreciate them. He had the opportunity to regularly visit the museum, which was located in his town's castle, admiring old furniture, sculptures and of course paintings. Those experiences and the mysterious swamps surrounding Leczyca had a huge impact on his work and life. The darkness of dungeons and legends about the greatest guardian of Lenczyca's treasure - Devil Boruta - appears in his works quite often. From that time until today, he uses oil paints and many old master techniques of his influences (John Martin, Rembrandt, Rubens, Van Dyke) to create his own magical world of imagination and dreams about life and death in the atmosphere of mystery. In 1986 he left Poland for Rome, Italy where he painted and lived for 2 years. Most of his work was purchased by critic and art lover Mario Tesorio. After 2 years he moved to Canada, where for 13 years he has displayed his works in several art Galleries as well as working in the motion picture industry. In 2003 he moved to beautiful Vancouver, British Columbia, where he lives today.